ARCHAEOLOGY FOR
EUROPE

TOP ARCHAEOLOGICAL DIG SITES AND DISCOVERIES
GUIDE ON ARCHAEOLOGICAL ARTIFACTS
5TH GRADE SOCIAL STUDIES

BABY PROFESSOR
EDUCATION KIDS

Speedy Publishing LLC

40 E. Main St. #1156

Newark, DE 19711

www.speedypublishing.com

Copyright 2017

In this book, we're going to talk about some of the top archaeological dig sites in Europe. So, let's get right to it!

STONEHENGE, ENGLAND

Located in the county of Wiltshire in the country of England, Stonehenge is one of the most famous archaeological sites in the world.

It is a ring of enormous stones that are standing upright. There are at least 900 of these stone rings throughout the British Isles, but Stonehenge is the most well known.

Most archaeologists agree that Stonehenge dates back to somewhere between 2000 through 3000 BC and was built about 300 years prior to the Egyptian pyramids.

However, ancient peoples buried the cremated remains of their dead in the same location, before the stones were erected, over 5,000 years ago.

Archaeologists have estimated that it may have taken as many as 30 million hours of work over a span of 1500 years to build. Two different types of stone were used at the site.

The larger stones are called sarsens and the smaller ones are bluestones, which had to be transported from at least 250 kilometers away. Inside the enclosure, there is a circle made up of 56 pits, named Aubrey Holes, after John Aubrey who first discovered them in 1666 AD. It's believed that these holes held posts or stones, but their purpose isn't known.

Because Stonehenge has been around for many thousands of years, artifacts from many different eras have been found there. Pottery and metal coins from the Roman Empire have been dug up from sites located there and some items from medieval times have been discovered there as well.

ROMAN COINS

There are no written records that provide historical data about Stonehenge, so everything that is known about it has come from archaeological studies. There are still so many mysteries about the site. No one knows how the heavy stones were transported at such great distances to the site.

There are some stones that are placed on top of two stones. These stones weigh many tons so the builders must have had sophisticated methods to lift and position them.

There have been many theories on how Stonehenge was used. Some believe it was used as a place for worship. Others believe that it was used for human sacrifices or as a place for ceremonies related to burial. The site may have been a type of ancient clock or astronomical observatory.

POMPEII, ITALY

In 79 AD, the city of Pompeii in the country of Italy was a major resort for wealthy Roman people who would vacation in their second homes there during the hot summers. Pompeii was laid out as many other Roman cities.

THE FORUM

The forum was located on[1] one side of the city. This was the location where most of the commerce was carried out. There were also temples to the many Roman gods, such as Venus and Apollo.

Arched aqueducts transported water to the center of the city for use in decorative fountains and large public baths. Some of the wealthy even had running water to use inside their homes.

THE COLOSSEUM

The city of Pompeii had a huge outdoor theater called an amphitheater like the Colosseum in Rome. More than 20,000 people could be seated there to watch gladiators fight against each other. There were other theaters for watching plays, musical presentations, and religious rituals.

About 17 years before Pompeii was stopped in time, there was an enormous earthquake that destroyed much of the city. Rebuilding was still in progress when the disaster hit.

POMPEII

The ancient Romans didn't realize that this earthquake and others like it were a signal of magma building under the active volcano that was nearby.

MOUNT VESUVIUS

Just one day after their religious ceremony honoring the god of fire, Vulcan, Mount Vesuvius exploded with a force that was one hundred thousand times more powerful than the atom bomb that exploded over Hiroshima. The cloud of ash over the volcano was twenty miles high with over 1.5 million tons being spewed out every second during the eruption. Some people had become nervous about the preliminary smoke emerging from the volcano and they left in time. However, over 16,000 people were killed when the volcano erupted.

Although it was a terrible disaster, when the site was discovered by archaeologists in the 1700s, it was an amazing find. As they began to excavate, they found buildings of all types, workshops, paintings, and other works of art that had been preserved in time under the piles of ash. There were also holes left in the ashes where bodies had been buried during the eruption.

POMPEII

When they poured plaster into these holes, they discovered the exact position people were in when they died. A great deal of the knowledge we have about how people lived during the Roman Empire comes from the archaeological digs at Pompeii.

ACROPOLIS, GREECE

The terrain in Greece is very mountainous and to defend themselves from invaders the Greek people designed their cities to be situated on rocky sections of land that stood above the surrounding land.

There are many of these outcroppings in Greece, but the most famous of them all is the Acropolis, which essentially means "city on a high hill."

ACROPOLIS

Located in what was the city-state of Athens during ancient Greek times, the Acropolis is situated 150 meters above sea level. The site was used by ancient peoples as early as the Neolithic Period, which was around 10,000 BC.

However, the most important buildings constructed there were built from 495 BC through 429 BC. This was the "Golden Age of Pericles" when peace and great abundance belonged to the citizens of Athens. Pericles commissioned the construction of the most famous building, the Parthenon, a temple to their patron goddess Athena, which was actually built on top of a much older temple structure.

THE PARTHENON

In 480 BC, the Persians invaded Athens and attacked the city. Some of the buildings were damaged in the attack and many sacred and artistic objects were destroyed. The Athenians recovered some of these when the attack was over and they carefully buried the jars, votives, and vases. They did this with such care that it has provided a treasure trove for archaeologists to find. These artifacts are called the "Persian Debris."

The buildings on the Acropolis, such as the Erechtheion, with its gigantic statues and ionic columns, as well as the Temple of Athena Nike, have been undergoing major restoration for the last four decades.

Hundreds of experts in fields as diverse as archaeology, marble working, and structural engineering have been working together to restore these ancient treasures to their previous glory.

ERECHTHEION

MONTIGNAC

LASCAUX CAVE PAINTINGS, FRANCE

In 1940, close to the city of Montignac in France, four teenagers were pursuing their dog when he ran into a cavern. When they went after him down the narrow passageway, they made a startling discovery. Deep inside were amazing prehistoric paintings of animals.

Eventually, the paintings were dated and it was found that they were at least 15,000 to 17,000 years old. They were some of the most beautiful and detailed paintings ever discovered from the Upper Paleolithic Period.

LASCAUX PAINTING

GROTTE DE LASCAUX

The cavern, called the Lascaux grotto, has a main area that is 66 feet in width and 16 feet in height. The cavern's walls are covered with a huge number of paintings and drawings. The prehistoric art expert and archaeologist, Henri-Édouard-Prosper Breuil, came to the site to authenticate the paintings as true originals created by ancient peoples.

He had studied the art of this time period for such a long time that he was able to recognize certain stylistic techniques to verify their age. The paintings, as well as the etchings, were deemed by Breuil to be authentic.

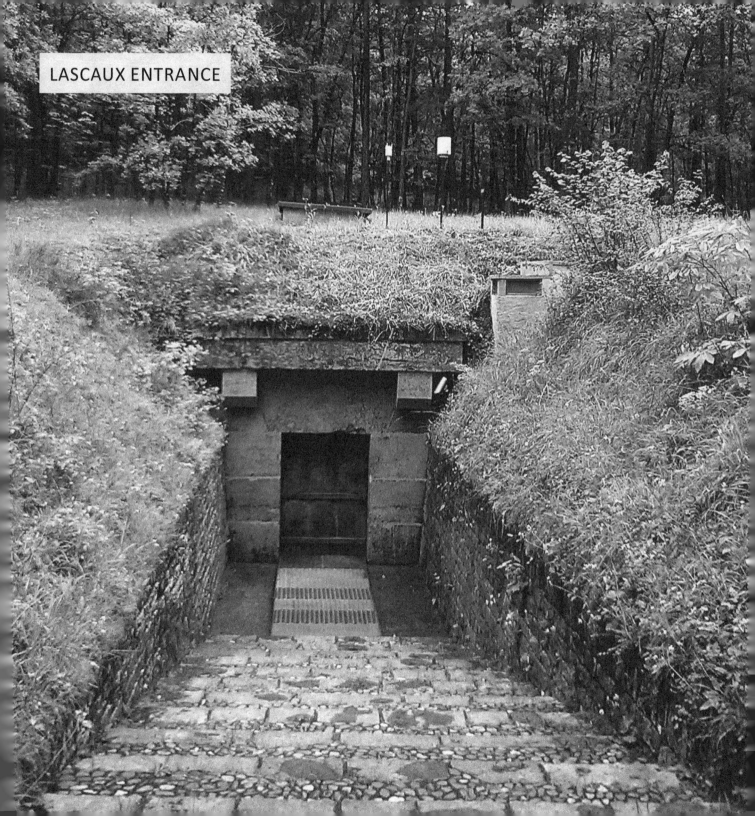

LASCAUX ENTRANCE

The art shows all different varieties of animals including red deer and stags as well as horses, bovines, and wild cats. Many of them are shown in dynamic running positions. Some of the animals are imaginary creatures. Surprisingly, there is only one man shown in all of the paintings and engravings and he has a bird's head. There are over 600 animals and symbols in all.

Originally the grotto was open for public view, but the beautiful, bright colors of the animals were becoming destroyed both by algae and by the artificial lighting placed there so that people could view them. Archaeologists think that the location was used for centuries for special rituals related to hunting. The depictions may have had spiritual significance as well.

SUMMARY

Sometimes, disasters in ancient times provide priceless artifacts that archaeologists find to make amazing discoveries thousands of years later. A burial site in England, a giant graveyard of ash in Italy, and a city under attack in Athens, Greece were all different types of tragedies in their day, but today provide valuable clues for archaeologists to find as they piece together information about the ancient civilizations of Europe.

Awesome! Now that you've read about some of the interesting archaeological finds in Europe you may want to read about archaeological sites in Asia in the Baby Professor book Archaeology for Kids – Asia –Top Archaeological Dig Sites and Discoveries.

CPSIA information can be obtained
at www.ICGtesting.com
Printed in the USA
BVHW061952220722
642587BV00004B/220

9 781541 916692